VOCAL SELECTIONS

MYTHS AND H

Music by Adam Guettel

Original Lyrics by Adam Guettel

Additional Lyrics by Ellen Fitzhugh

Cover design by Barbara de Wilde, from Herbert James Draper's "Lament for Icarus" (1898), courtesy of the Tate Gallery, London.

ISBN 0-634-01786-1

www.williamsonmusic.com

EXCLUSIVELY DISTRIBUTED BY

7777 W. BLUEMOUND RD. P.O. BOX 13819 MILWAUKEE, WI 53213

Many of these songs are adapted from Greek myths and from lyrics I found in an old hymnal in a used bookshop. I used these dissimilar cosmologies as points of departure and discovered as I went along that they have a lot in common—a desire to transcend earthly bounds, to bond with something or someone greater. They seem to complement each other, reflecting different parts of us: the myths, our behaviors; the hymns, our prayers.

— ADAM GUETTEL
New York City, 1999

Very often, therefore, in human affairs we are subject to Saturn, through idleness, solitude, or strength, through Theology and more secret philosophy, through superstition, Magic, agriculture, and through sadness.

— MARSILIO FICINO (1433–1499)
from *The Book of Life*

ADAM GUETTEL is a composer/lyricist living in New York City. Recent work includes LOVE'S FIRE, a collaboration with John Guare for The Acting Company, and SATURN RETURNS, a concert at Joseph Papp Public Theater/New York Shakespeare Festival. SATURN RETURNS was recorded by Nonesuch Records under the title MYTHS AND HYMNS, released in March 1999. Four of Mr. Guettel's songs are featured on Audra McDonald's 1998 Nonesuch Records release, WAY BACK TO PARADISE. Recent work also includes music and lyrics for FLOYD COLLINS (also on Nonesuch Records) at Playwrights Horizons (1996), the score for ARGUING THE WORLD, a recent feature documentary by Joe Dorman at the Film Forum, NY, and the score for JACK, a two-hour documentary for CBS by Peter Davis (1994). In Spring 1999, FLOYD COLLINS was presented at The Old Globe Theater in San Diego, The Prince Theatre (American Music Theatre Festival) in Philadelphia, and The Goodman Theater in Chicago. It was given its U.K. premiere at The Bridewell Theatre, London, in July 1999.

Mr. Guettel is currently working on a love story, as yet untitled. He is the recipient of the Stephen Sondheim Award (1990), the Obie Award (1996), the Lucille Lortel Award (1996), and the ASCAP New Horizons Award (1997). Adam Guettel performed a concert evening of his work at New York's Town Hall in May 1999.

CONTENTS

Prometheus

Music by
Adam Guettel

13
p
p
17
21
3
sim.
25
f
f

mp
mp

45
mp
f
mp

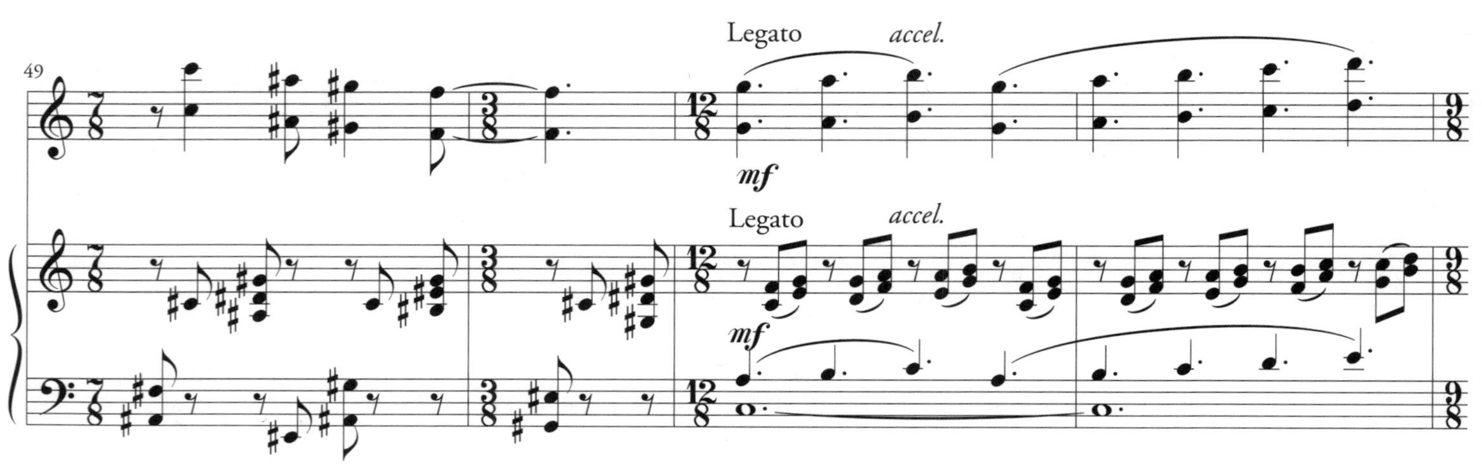
49
Legato
accel.
mf
Legato
accel.
mf

53
A tempo
accel.
rit.
cresc...
A tempo
accel.
rit.
cresc...

celebratory
A tempo
57
ff
celebratory
A tempo
ff
61
3
64
3

Saturn Returns

Music and Lyrics by
Adam Guettel

14
but now it's gone, and I am in - com-plete.
3
3
17
In the dark - ness, and the hol-low, in the heat.
20
mp
If I flash on the fu - ture, there is on-ly the emp - ty fu-ture shock, an af-ter-im - age.
3
mp
23
There is on-ly I want, I want, I want. I
accel.
cresc.

(♩ = 70)
25
don't know what I hun - ger for, I don't know why I feel the hun - ger more
mf
27
and more with ev - 'ry pass - ing day.
29
I don't know from where the hun - ger springs, but that it's there and that it sings
(♮)
31
of some - place far a - way.
(♩ = 60)
rit.
decresc.
p
5
4

34
p
ten.
So get me up, and get me out, and let me nev-er re - turn to the dark -
ten.
ten.
36
- ness, and the hol-low and to the burn. I want out of this hun - ger,
39
3
take me up to a high - er al - ti - tude. Take me all the way! I'm out
41
3
of here. I am go - ing there. I am gone!
molto cresc.
f

44
pp
mf
pp
mf
pp
mf
f
(♮)
47
mf
And now...
p
f
accel.
I am
8vb
(♩ = 70)
50
the rise of Ic - a - rus, I am the fall from Peg - a - sus. I am
ff
(8vb)
52
the lost Le - an - der in the tide.
decresc.
mp
loco
(♮)

54
I am cold, a-lone, and set a-part and I am warm as He - ro's heart.
cresc
56
I am a cir - cle I am Sat - urn pur - i-fied!
58
Once a-round the sun and now at last I see it!
rit.
60
(♩ = 60)
This is what I am!
f
f
p

63
p
Long a-go I left my-self and now I try — to re - turn As a strang -
p
p

66
mp
- er to a strange land — and to the burn. But the hol - low in - side — me
mp

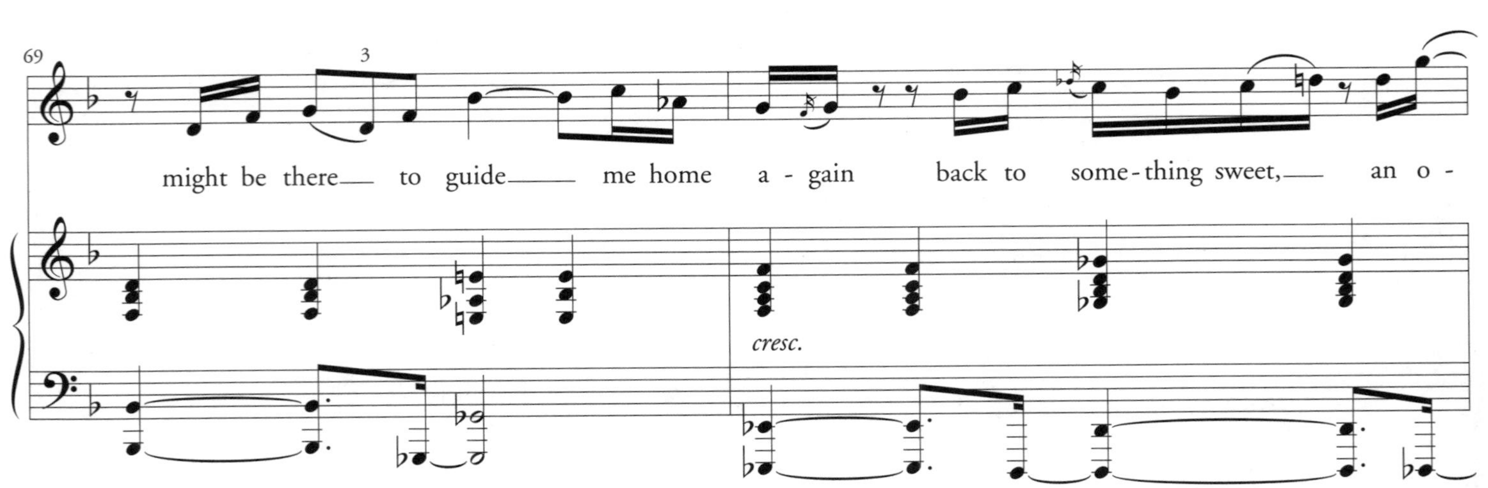
69
3
might be there — to guide — me home a - gain back to some - thing sweet, — an o -
cresc.

71
pen - ing
A pas
sage - way
to guide
Gradual accel
73
(♩ = 64)
me
home!
rit.
75
rit.

Icarus

Music and Lyrics by
Adam Guettel

14
I
His fa - ther trust - ed him and took it for grant - ed
16
I
That he would turn out to be just as en - chant - ed;
18
I
That all he need - ed was some help get - ting off the ground..
DAEDALUS:
20
D
Put these on and learn to fly a course a - bove the o - cean.

24
D
Test your strength. Learn to change the an-gle of your wing.
But,
28
D
Ic - a-rus, fly be-neath me, shad-ed from the sun.
32
D
Un - lim-it-ed al-ti-tude will heat up your wings and they'll
35
D
come un - glued. Of the sun, you must be - ware

37
D
when you're glid - ing through the air.
You have to try to stay in my
39
B/U
BACK-UP
Ba da da Ba da da Ba da da
ICARUS:
I
Ic-a-rus could see the po-ten - tial
Aer-o-dy-nam - ic myth - o - log-i - cal coup
D
sha - dow
42
B/U
Ba da da Ba da da
I
Of being the on - ly fly - ing de - mi god who

44
B/U
Da
da
I
Dared to land on the sun.
46
B/U
Ba da da Ba da da
I
Ic - a - rus could see the cre - den - tial
48
B/U
Ba da da Ba da da
I
And face the glo - ry of the jour - ney a - head.

50
B/U
I
Ba da da Ba da da
The light re - flect - ed off his wings when they spread.
52
Ah
ICARUS:
He start - ed sing - ing when his feet on - ly found air.
54
Look at me. I'm going to be the stuff that myths are made of. Di-

58
vine e-vent; The kind of myth that makes a mas-que - rade of a fa-ther.
62
O - ver him, I'll cast a shad-ow broad-er than the sun.
66
Un - lim - i - ted al-ti - tude; I like to nav-i-gate
69
in the nude. Breez - es blow - ing through my hair

71
I
while I ride the dunes of air.
I think I'll let him fly in my
73
B/U
He didn't try to get his ears to pop.
He liked the at-mos-pher-ic pres-sure drop
I
shad - ow.
75
B/U
The sky a-round him and the earth be-low,
the earth be - low...
earth be - low...
Guitar solo
Gtr

78
B/U
earth be - low...
earth be - low...
earth be - low...
Gtr
81
B/U
earth be - low...
earth be - low...
earth be - low...
Gtr
84
B/U
earth be - low...
earth be - low...
earth be - low...
earth be - low...
Gtr

88
B/U
ICARUS & DAEDALUS:
Di-
I/D
Look at me. I'm going to be the stuff that myths are made of. Di-
92
B/U
vine e-vent; The kind of myth that makes a mas-que-rade of a fa-ther.
I/D
vine e-vent; The kind of myth that makes a mas-que-rade of a fa-ther.
96
O - ver him, I'll cast a shad-ow broad-er than the sun.
O - ver him, I'll cast a shad-ow broad-er than the sun.

100
B/U
Ah!
ICARUS:
I
Un - lim-i-ted al-ti-tude; The o - zone lay-er is rain-bow hued..
104
I
Nim-bus cloud a-bout my head I think I'll wear it in my fa-ther's stead.
DAEDALUS:
D
I think the air is get - ting
107
B/U
Di-
ICARUS:
I
Look at me. I'm going to be the stuff that myths are made of. Di-
D
thin. I'm going to be the stuff that myths are made of. Di-

111
B/U
vine e - vent; The kind of myth that makes a mas - que - rade of a
ICARUS & DAEDALUS:
I/D
vine e - vent; The kind of myth that makes a mas - que - rade of a
114
B/U
fa - ther. O - ver him I'll
ICARUS:
I
fa - ther. Bee - yoot - n - doot - doot O - ver him I'll
116
B/U
cast a shad - ow broad - er than the sun.
I
cast a shad - ow broad - er than the sun.

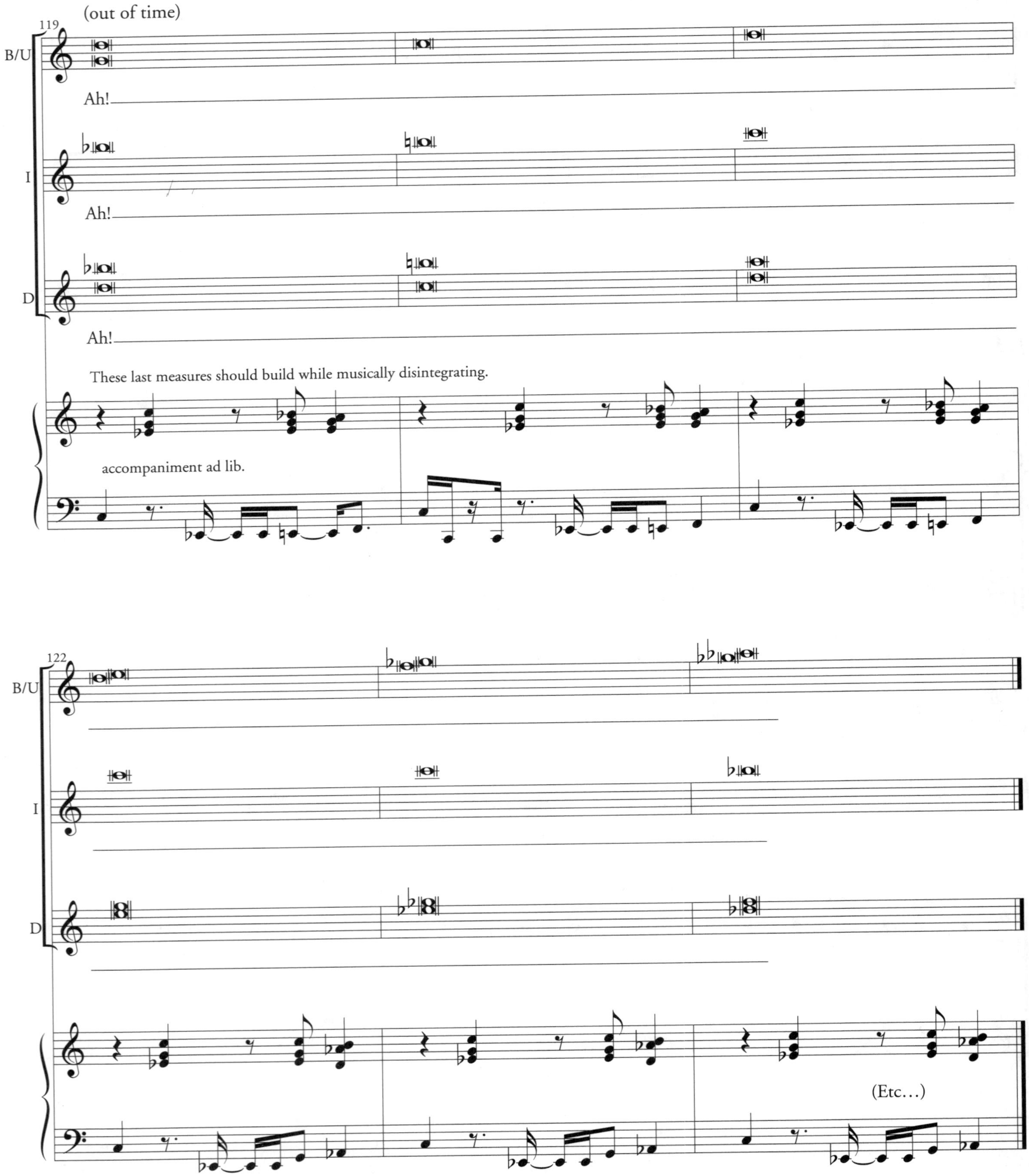

(out of time)

119

B/U

Ah!

I

Ah!

D

Ah!

These last measures should build while musically disintegrating.

accompaniment ad lib.

Migratory V

Music and Lyrics by
Adam Guettel

Contemplative (♩. = 72)

16
sail a - bove the weath - er
We
mp
20
search the o - cean floor
We
24
riv - al our cre - a - tion
still
28
yearn - ing for more
But

32
can we fly to - geth - er a
36
mi - gra - tor - y V How
40
won - der - ful if that's what God could
44
see A sin - gle voice in whis - pered prayer can on - ly

48
pray to trav - el there but all as one we sound the
51
ev - er - last - ing sound, and sing our sal - va - tion. A -
8vb
54
loft and in for - ma - tion a mi - gra -
mf
57
tor - y V How won - der - ful if
ff

60
that's
what God
could
see.
3
p

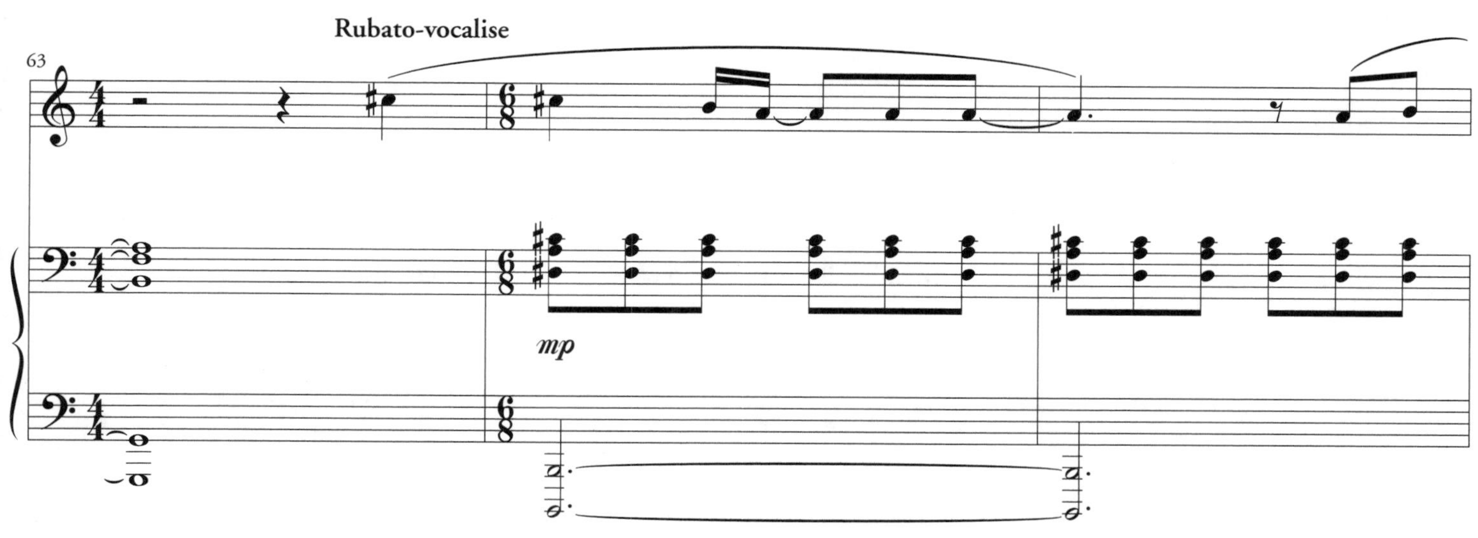
Rubato-vocalise
63
mp

66
8vb

Pegasus

Music and Lyrics by Adam Guettel
Additional Lyrics by Ellen Fitzhugh

18
Peg - a - sus, I meant to glow like you glow:
22
Up in Heav-en too, Heav-en like you got. In the wind your fly-ing mane,
25
In my hand your gold - en rein.
28
High - er, higher and nev-er too high and nev-er e - nough.

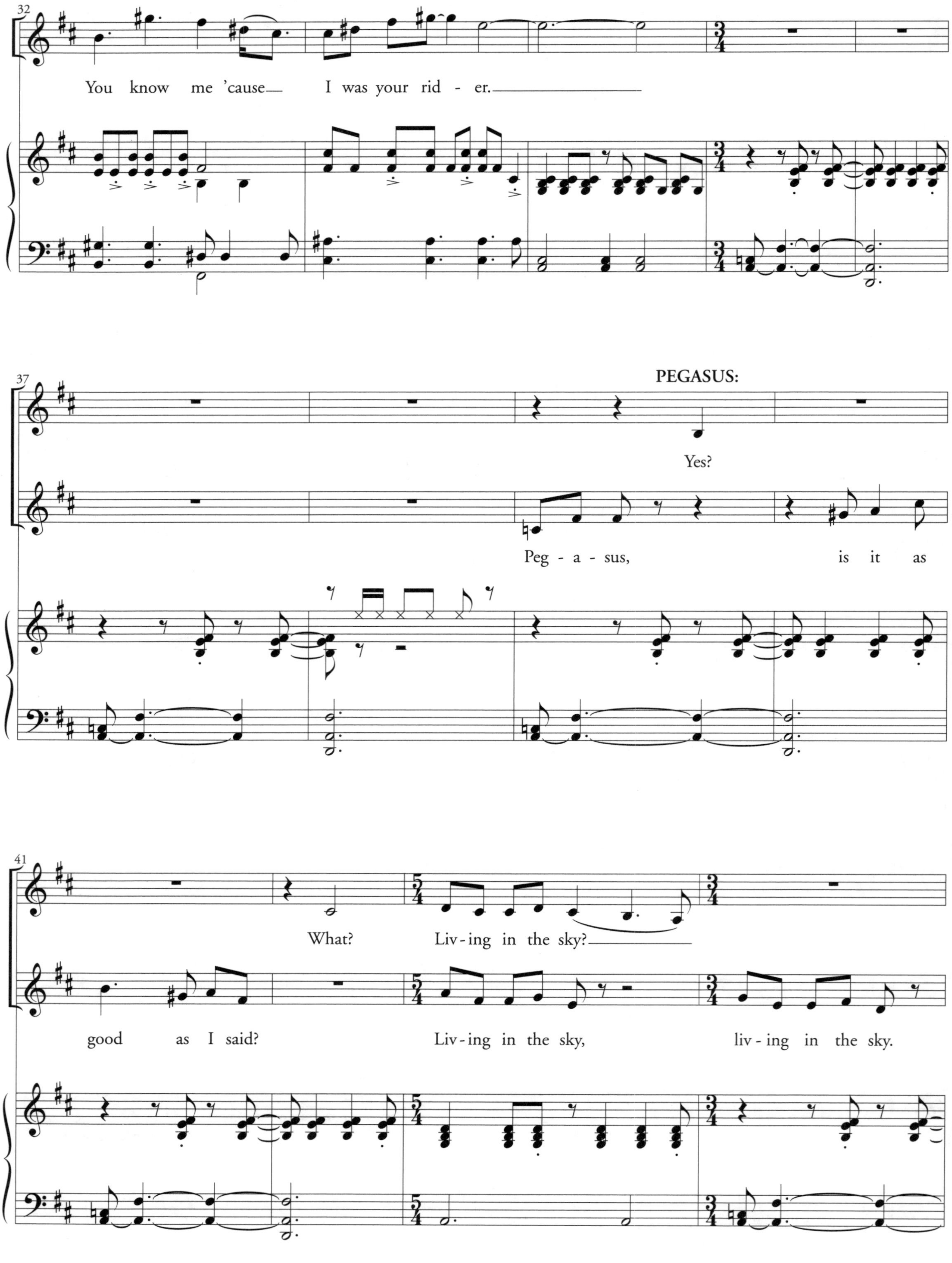

32

You know me ’cause— I was your rid - er.—

37

PEGASUS:

Yes?

Peg - a - sus, is it as

41

45
Well...
Uh - huh?
Peg - a - sus,
49
What dance? Heav-en like you got ain't liv-ing in the sky.
there was a dance on your head.
Heav-en like you got
liv-ing in the sky.
5
4
54
Af-ter ris - ing from the blood...
pret - ty!
Af-ter drink-ing from the
Af - ter ris - ing from the blood...
Af - ter drink - ing from the

57
flood
Higher - er, higher, and nev - er too high, and nev-er e - nough.
flood
Higher - er, higher, and nev - er too high and nev-er e - nough.
61
Tell them how you threw your rid - er.
65
GADFLY:
Brr - ip bu-bu brr - ip bu-bu bu-bu-bu-bu-bzz-ip Bu-bu-bu-bu-bu-bu-brr - ip brr - ip bu-bu-bu-bu-bzz-ip

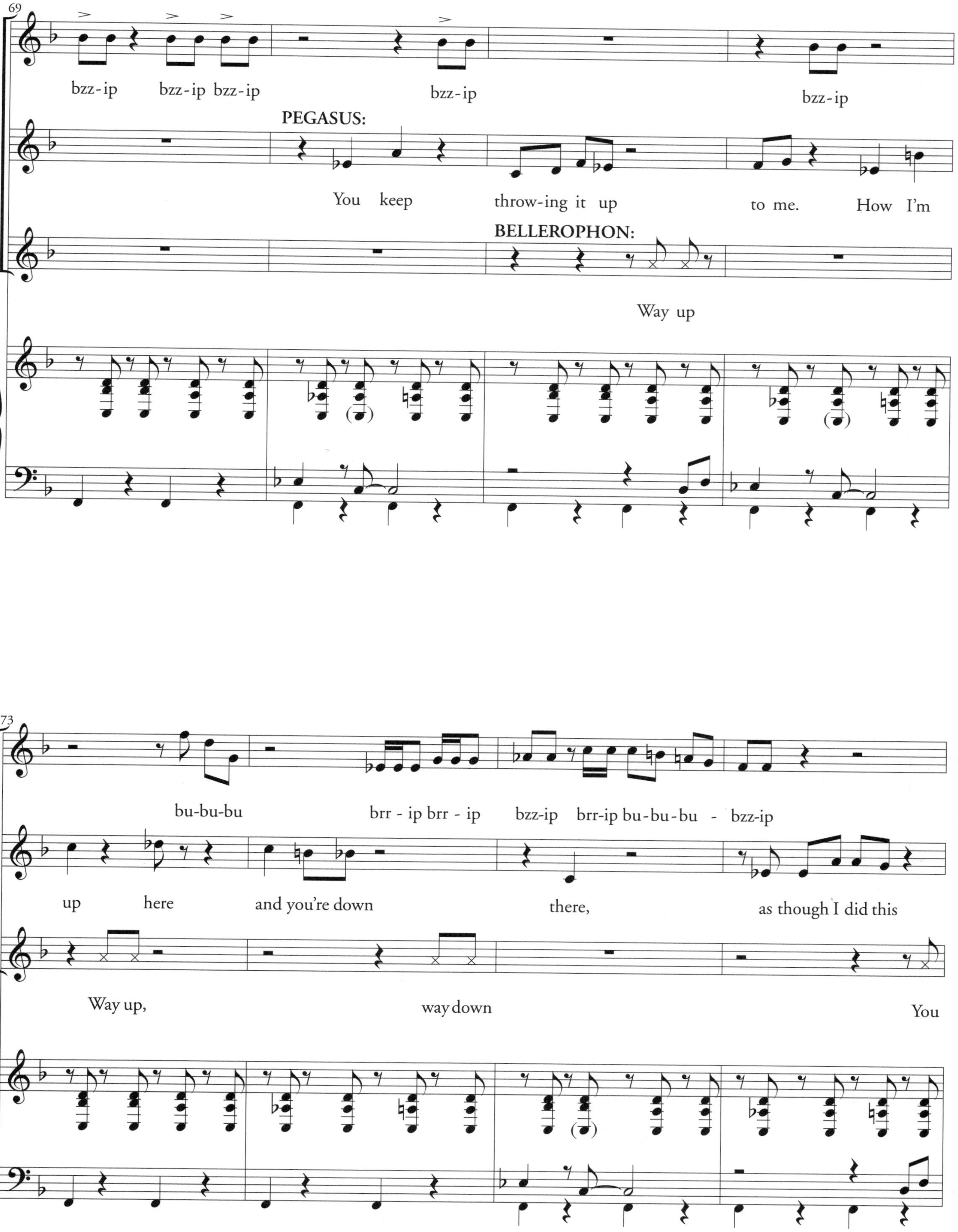

69

bzz-ip bzz-ip bzz-ip bzz-ip bzz-ip

PEGASUS:

You keep throw-ing it up to me. How I'm

BELLEROPHON:

Way up

77
f
A gad - fly does - n't much deal
to you..
did this to me.
Lazy shuffle
81
in re - gret, For a gad - fly there is no re - morse.
86
A gad - fly does - n't much ques - tion her God

91
When her God___ says: "Go bite that fly - ing horse!"___ She
5
95
bites. That's it. I bit.
PEGASUS:
Brr - ip bu - bu brr - ip bu - bu
(SLAP!)
99
bu - bu - bu - bu - bzz - ip now I hear this one
PEGASUS:
I think

102
blames
and that one blames.
They each make
you must-'ve pinched
my flank...
Some-how
pinched
me,
BELLEROPHON:
I pinched?
I pinched?

105
claims
and
coun-ter-claims.
They
seize up-on
the in-ci-dent,
and
I flinched.
Flinched.
You bucked.

108
GADFLY:
Look for im-pli-ca-tions. When it was on - ly Zeus a-gain vent-ing his frus-tra-tions.
111
PEGASUS:
Why
I did-n't throw you. You lie!
BELLEROPHON:
You threw me. You lie!
115
this? Why this?
That's my name... Broke in two.
Peg - a sus, We broke in two.

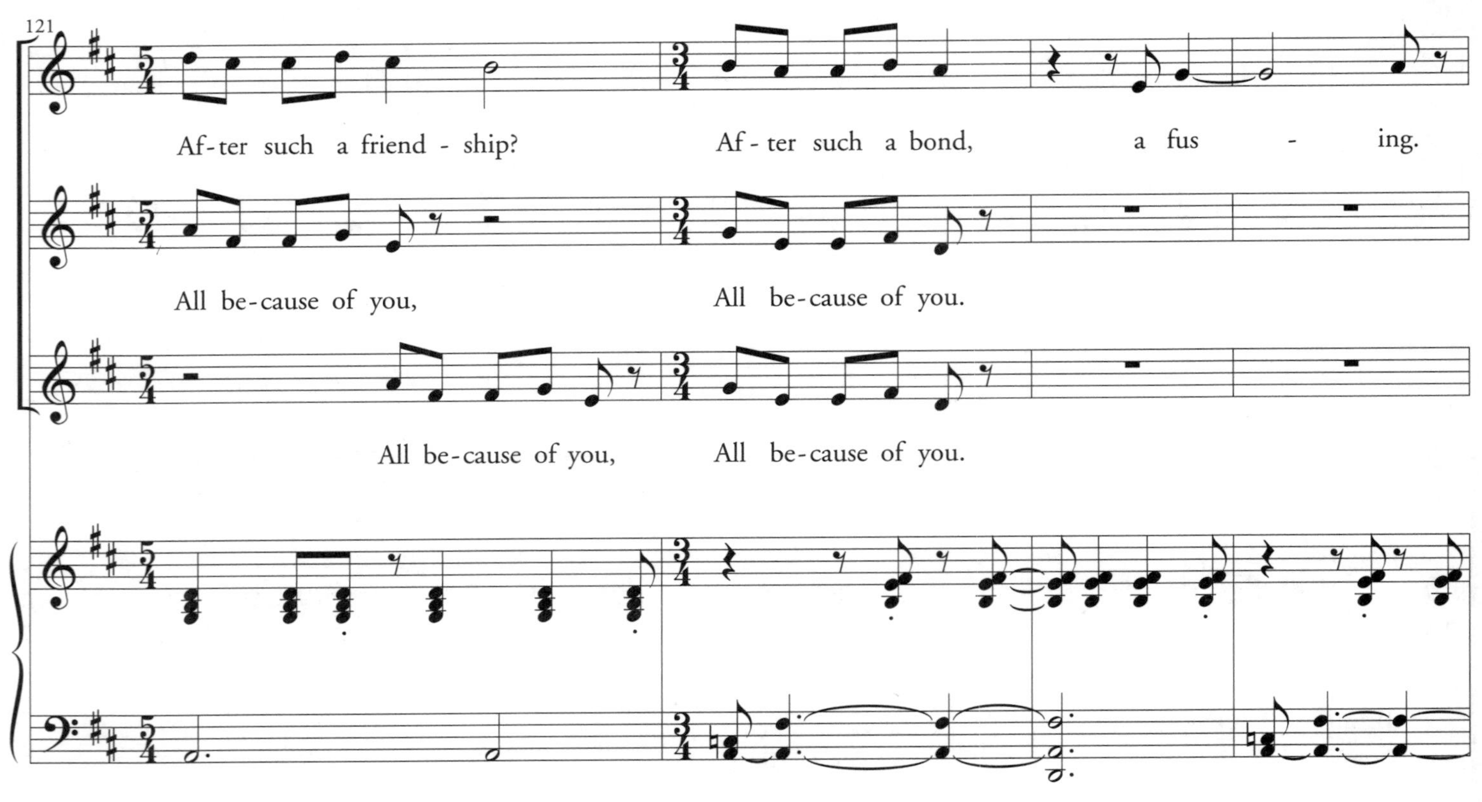
121
Af-ter such a friend - ship? Af - ter such a bond, a fus - ing.
All be-cause of you, All be-cause of you.
All be-cause of you, All be-cause of you.

125
Why this?
Peg - a - sus, just say it's true, say it's true.

129
More – than a friend-ship,
More – than a bond.
Rid-er and the horse in
I say it was you,
I say it was you.
I say it was you,
I say it was you.
You and I we still could go...

133
flight,
Weld-ed to the oth-er tight.
High - er, higher and
No, we won't, we'll nev-er go.
Nev - er will be so.
High - er, higher and
Say it, say it, say it will be so.
High - er, higher and

137
never too high, and never enough.
never too high, and never enough.
cresc.
never too high, and never enough. Olympians please

141
f A warm bloom here
Or must winged
f
Or must winged
f
make this pox be gone. Or must winged
f

145
And relax
Peg - a - sus
and down - ward - bound Bel -
Peg - a - sus
and down - ward - bound Bel -
Peg - a - sus
and down - ward - bound Bel -

149
mp
mf
ler - o - phon
That's it.
I bit.
ler - o - phon
go on?
ler - o - phon
go on?
6

Jesus the Mighty Conqueror

Music and Lyrics by
Adam Guettel

13
doth re-veal to mor - tals the tri-umphs of His might. For the Lord
17
hath ris - en. The Lord hath ris - en, and con - quered ev - 'ry foe.
20
The Lord hath ris - en, The Lord hath ris - en so!
23
Rise
Bubbling texture, out of rhythm

27
Rise
The grave its aw - ful con - quest O'er
31
man for ag - es won,
De - feat - ed, now sur - ren - ders, to
35
God's vic-to-ri-ous son;
The might - y con - quer-or, cap - tive Now

39
leaves cap-tiv - i - ty,
Pre - cious gifts be - stow -
42
- ing
of life and lib - er - ty.
For the Lord
45
hath ris - en. The Lord hath ris - en, and con - quered ev - 'ry foe.

48

– The Lord hath ris - en, The Lord hath ris - en so!

CHORUS:

He's con-quered ev - 'ry foe Ris - en so

51

Rise

Rise

Bubbling texture, out of rhythm

54

61
pow - er for - ev - er is bro - ken, God's saints no long - er mourn,
64
Its sting can bring no tor - ture, For Christ the curse hath borne,
68
His glo - rious ex - alt - a - tion, Let

71
men and an - gels sing,
Je - sus the might - y con -
74
- quer-or
In earth and heav'n is King.
For the Lord

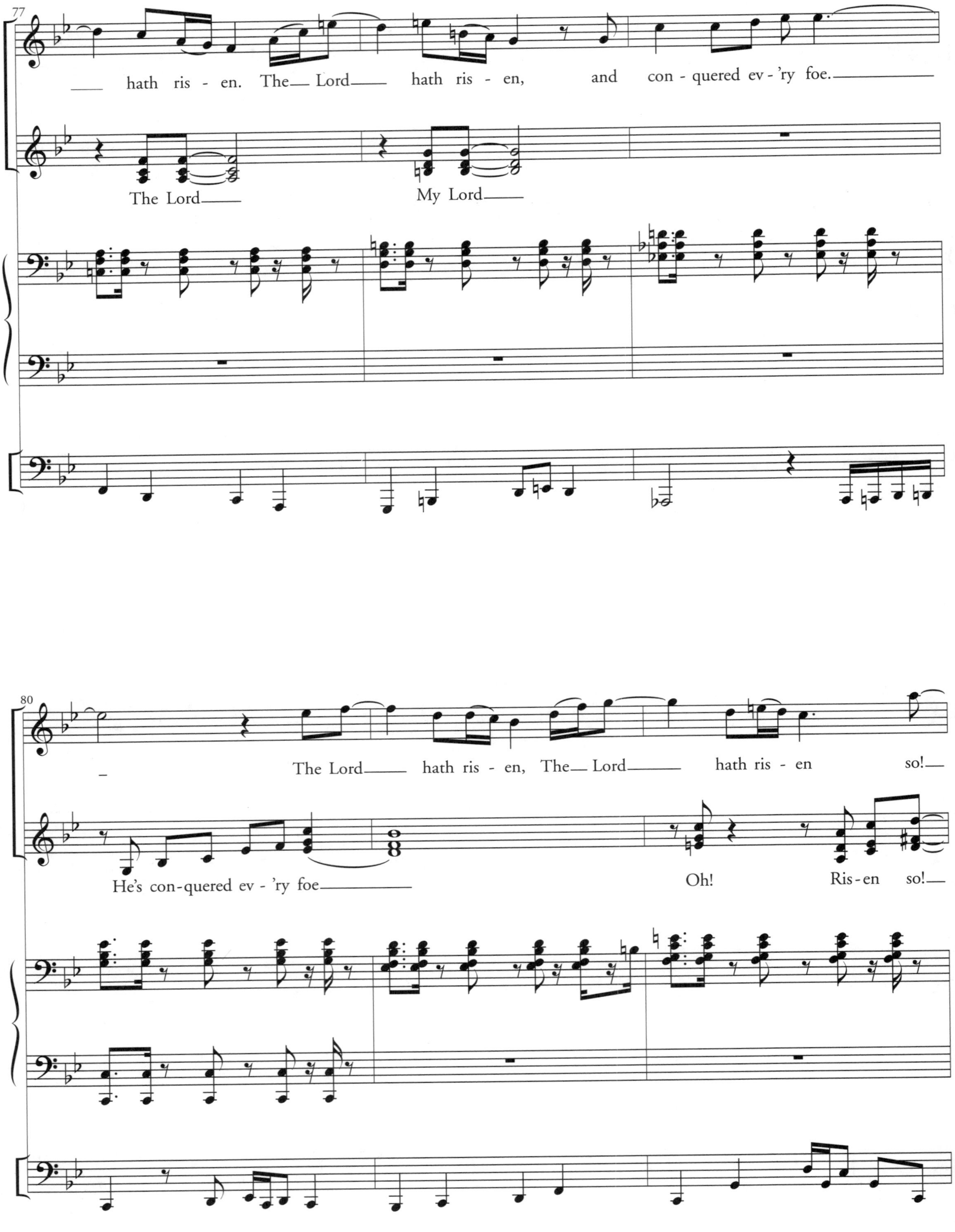

80

The Lord hath ris - en, The Lord hath ris - en so!

He's con - quered ev - 'ry foe

Oh! Ris - en so!

83
Rise
Rise
Bubbling texture, out of rhythm
86
Rise
Rise

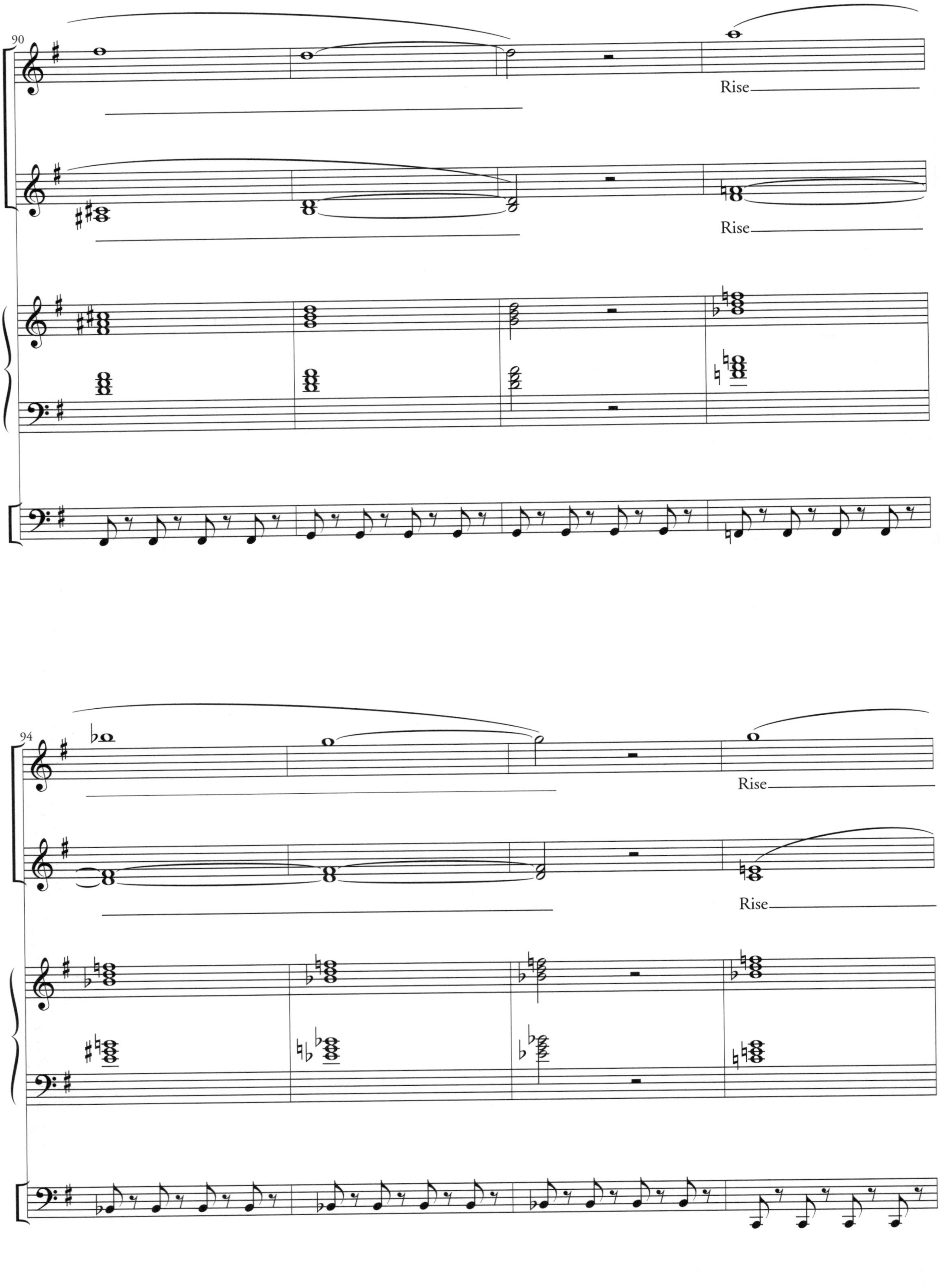

90

Rise

Rise

94

Rise

Rise

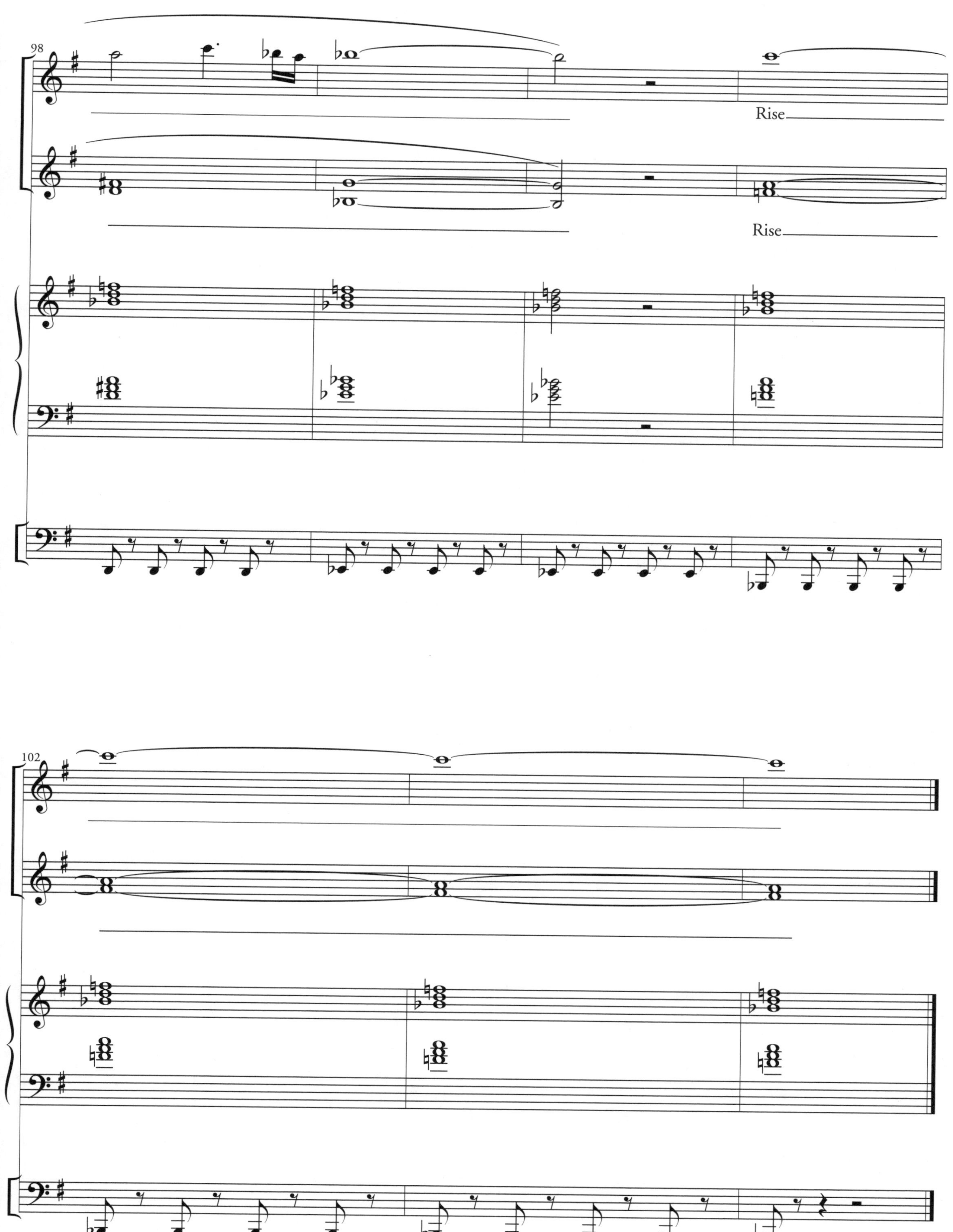
98
Rise
Rise
102

Children of the Heavenly King

Music and Lyrics by Adam Guettel
Lyrics adapted from
The Temple Trio, Hymn Edition, 1886

At the Sounding

Music and Lyrics by Adam Guettel
Lyrics adapted from
The Temple Trio, Hymn Edition, 1886

ff *loco* 8vb *sim.*

5

f

At the sound - ing of the trum - pet, when the saints are gath - ered

At the sound - ing of the trum - pet, when the saints are gath - ered

At the sound - ing of the trum - pet, when the saints are gath - ered

8

mp *f*

home, we will greet each oth - er by the crys - tal sea. With the

home, we will greet each oth - er by the crys - tal sea. With the

home, we will greet each oth - er by the crys - tal sea. With the

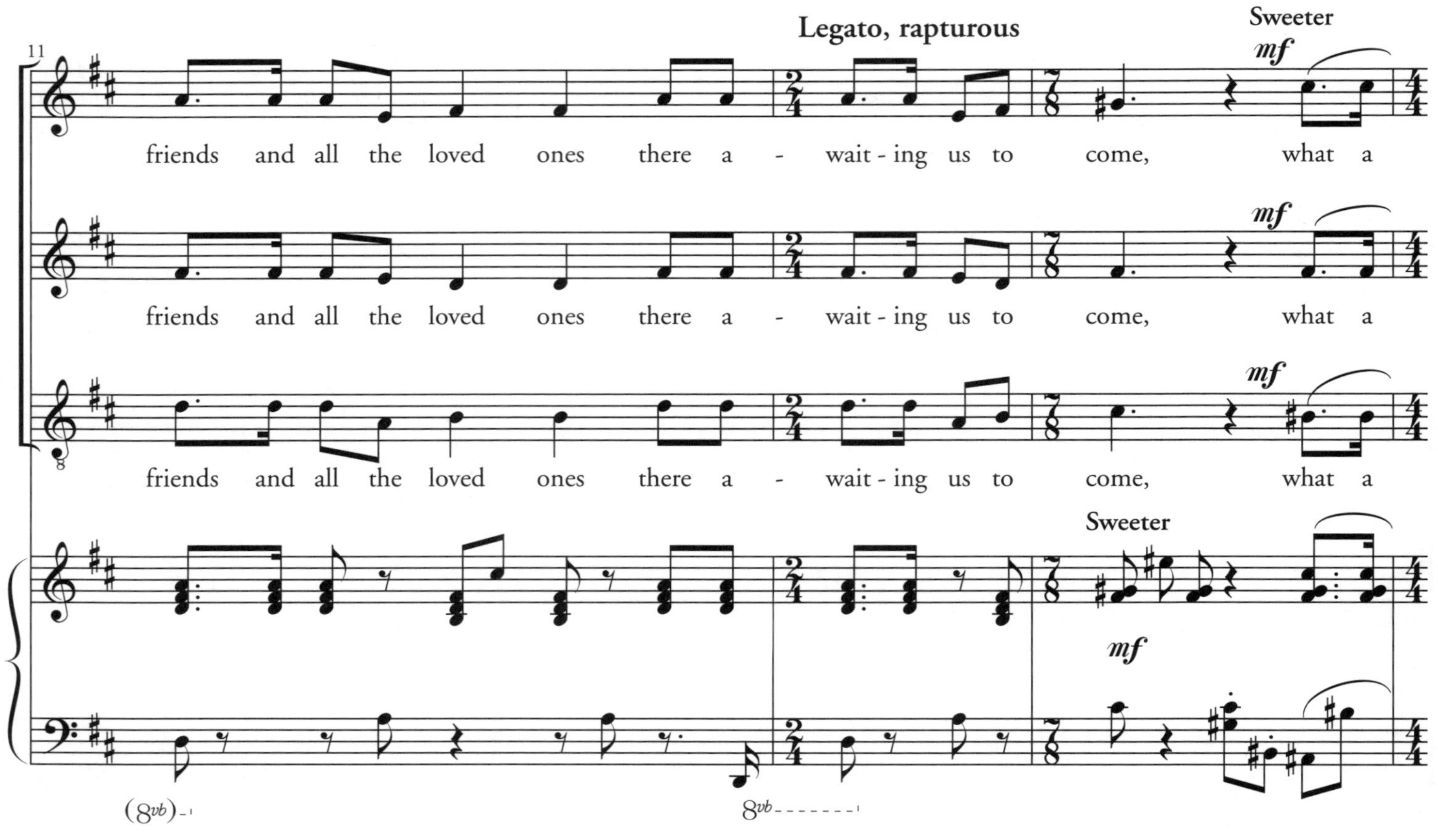

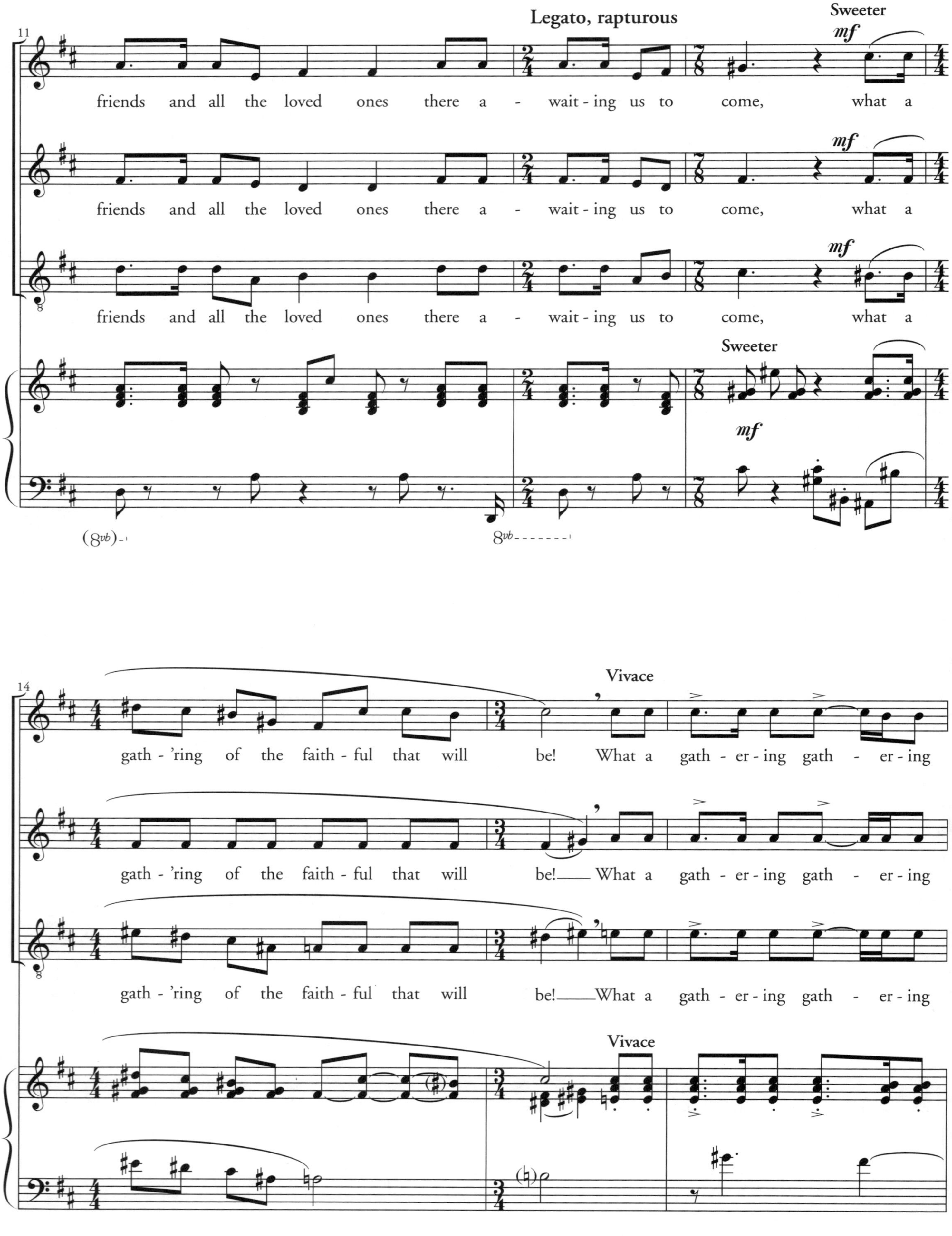
11
Legato, rapturous
Sweeter
mf
friends and all the loved ones there a - wait - ing us to come, what a
mf
friends and all the loved ones there a - wait - ing us to come, what a
mf
friends and all the loved ones there a - wait - ing us to come, what a
Sweeter
mf
(8vb)
8vb
14
Vivace
gath - 'ring of the faith - ful that will be! What a gath - er - ing gath - er - ing
gath - 'ring of the faith - ful that will be! What a gath - er - ing gath - er - ing
gath - 'ring of the faith - ful that will be! What a gath - er - ing gath - er - ing
Vivace

17
it will be at the sound - ing of the glor - i - ous ju - bil - ee! What a
it will be at the sound - ing of the glor - i - ous ju - bil - ee! What a
it will be at the sound - ing of the glor - i - ous ju - bil - ee! What a
21
f
gath - er - ing gath - er - ing it will be! What a gath - 'ring of the faith - ful that will be!
f
gath - er - ing gath - er - ing it will be! Gath - 'ring of the faith - ful that will be!
f
gath - er - ing gath - er - ing it will be! Gath - 'ring of the faith - ful that will be!
mf
Ah!
f
mf

Rhythmically precise rapture
25
Ah!
Ah!
Ah!
Ah!
Ah!
Ah!
Ah!
Ah!
sim.
cresc.
29
Ah!
Ah!
Ah!
Ah!
Ah!
Ah!
Ah!
Ah!
ff
8vb

Triumphant
ff
Ah!
Ah!
At the sound - ing of the trum - pet when the saints are gath - ered home,
At the sound - ing of the trum - pet when the saints are gath - ered home,
At the sound - ing of the trum - pet when the saints are gath - ered home,
(8vb)
8vb
8vb
Ah!
Ah!
when the gold - en harps are sound-ing and the an - gel bands pro - claim,
when the gold - en harps are sound-ing and the an - gel bands pro - claim,
when the gold - en harps are sound-ing and the an - gel bands pro - claim,
(8vb)
8vb

38
we will greet each oth - er by the
we will greet each oth - er by the
we will greet each oth - er by the
we will greet each oth - er by the
Ped.
40
mf
p
crys - tal sea. By the sea. Crys - tal sea.
crys - tal sea. By the sea. Crys - tal sea.
crys - tal sea. By the sea. Crys - tal sea.
crys - tal sea. By the sea. Crys - tal sea.
rall.
mf
p

Build a Bridge

Music and Lyrics by
Adam Guettel

15
ten.
shore. Build a bridge. This I've heard before.

18
Ah Ah I'll be
f
mf

22
com-ing... I am try-ing to get there, to bat-tle the wa-ter!

27
ten.
ten.
Build a bridge. Come to shore. Build a
32
bridge. This I've heard, how I have heard, so man - y times, for so man - y years gone
3
f
37
by.
Yes I
(Instrumental counter-melody)
ff
mf

41
need you, and I love you, but, oh, the wa-ter's wide. Oh, yes. I am

46
try-ing. I am try-ing to get there, to bat-tle the tide.

52
Repeat ad lib.
Oh, yes... I know.
fade out to taste
decresc...
mp

Sisyphus

Music and Lyrics by Adam Guettel
Additional Lyrics by Ellen Fitzhugh

20
optional
ag - ines it is... It is watch - ing while he's go - ing through this. (Heh-heh - heh-heh)
23
More up. Up more. If I fail then I try, try a - gain
Spare us. Free us. Free us. Spare us.
27
More more
Fail - ure Fail - ure still. Is the fail - ure the thrill?
sim.
30
Can't you see it's a curse!? Roll - ing rocks for - e - ver,
f

34
How could this be a curse? The
nev - er mere-ly be - ing dead.
38
ff
mf
rock sup-ply is end-less. And there's man-y a mil-len-ni-um
man-y a mil-len-ni-um
42
man - y a mil - len - ni - um a - head!
man - y a mil - len - ni - um a - head!
mp

44
Race ya to the rock pile! Gid - dy up! Tal - ly Ho! For-ward!
mf
46
Not al - lowed!
Do we have to? Can't we go?
48
You know what Zeus said... "I want Sis - y - phus to draw a nice
Zeus a - gain? Zeus a - gain! "I want Sis - y - phus to draw a nice

51
crowd."
Race ya to the rock pile!
crowd."
Gid - dy up! Tal - ly Ho! For - ward!
54
There's a point here. There's a point to be found.
I picked a dif - ferent
Stu - pid.
57
shape, size, rock.
Oops!
Oops, few lit - tle
Stu - pid. Stu - pid.
Rock rolls back and it-'ll flat - ten him flat.

60
bugs to work
Don't you e-ven be - gin to say that!
3
Trans - fer please to an - y-where
63
But I need you guys be - side me to ad -
else in this joint!
65
vise me and to guide me while I miss the whole point.

Life Is But a Dream

Music and Lyrics by
Adam Guettel

11
It's not e-nough, there must be more

14
Up-on a dis - tant shore
Ad-ven-ture and the thun - der of life

17
O - pen up your arms to me,
And I will find my way.

21
In my heart a rid - dle lives, And by the am - ber light it gives,
p

24
I will ask un - til I know who I am In - side the out -
poco rit. e cresc.
Slower
mp
f

27
- side that I show.
A tempo
mp

31
From where I sit it does - n't seem That life is but a dream It seems like there's a
mf
34
world out there.
poco rit. e cresc.
p
O - pen up your arms to me
A tempo
f
37
O - pen up your arms
And you will set me
8vb to end
41
free.
(trem.)

Hero and Leander

Music and Lyrics by
Adam Guettel

12
heart a-fire? My light-house on the shore-line, could you be that to me?
15
Oh I need you. I need the rise and fall of your voice.
ff
mf
18
Oh I love you, and now I have a love to re-joice.
ff
mf
21
He-ro and Le-an-der, how your pas-sion is brave,
f

* *A possible vocalise. Ad lib instead if you prefer.*

36
Oh
39
now, could you be that to me?
42
Oh, I need you. I need the rise and fall of your voice.
45
Oh, I love you. And now, I have a love to re-joice.

48
He-ro and Le-an-der, how your pas-sion is brave, e-ven if I drown here in-side
51
this wave. My light-house on the shore-line. My pas-sion on this
54
lone - ly sea My lov-ing you was meant,
58
was meant to be.

Come to Jesus

Music and Lyrics by Adam Guettel
Lyrics adapted from
The Temple Trio, Hymn Edition, 1886

Rubato, colla voce

EMILY:

p

Dear - est Mat - thew, I am writ - ing you from the wait - ing room I'm next.

p legato

10
I know we'd laugh if you were here in spite of ev - 'ry - thing.
14
Oh Mat - thew let's not let this tear us a - part I be - lieve this
17
lit - tle soul will cra - dle cra - dle in heav - en
3
20
un - til the day we can ac - cept him to - geth - er to -
3

22
3
geth - er for you and for me and for the child I pray.
Rhapsodic, hypnotic
26
mf
Come
mf
29
to Je - sus
32
Come to Je - sus

35
Come to Je - sus just
38
No vibrato
now
Just now come to Je - sus
41
Come to Je - sus just now
44
He will

47
save you
49
He will save you
52
He will save you just now
No vibrato
56
Just now He will save you

58
He will save you just now
61
More rubato
64
a tempo
Oh, be - lieve him He is a - ble He is will - ing
67
He'll re - ceive you Flee to Je - sus Call un - to Him

70
MATTHEW:
f
mf
p
Dear Em-i-ly I write from the air - port
73
Go-ing a-way for a while I could-n't love you like you want-ed but I did love you
76
gradual cresc.
I do It's just that af - ter what has hap-pened

79
something's ruined
You feel it too
dying
and I can't
mp
82
mf
look any-more.
To love
is to be accompanied,
guided by an angel
3
mf
85
but I've driven it away
And we are alone
88
now.
mp
Maybe you're right...
Maybe that soul will cradle in
mp

91
p
heav - en
and will
come to you one day
for that and for for - give -

94
ness I pray
mf

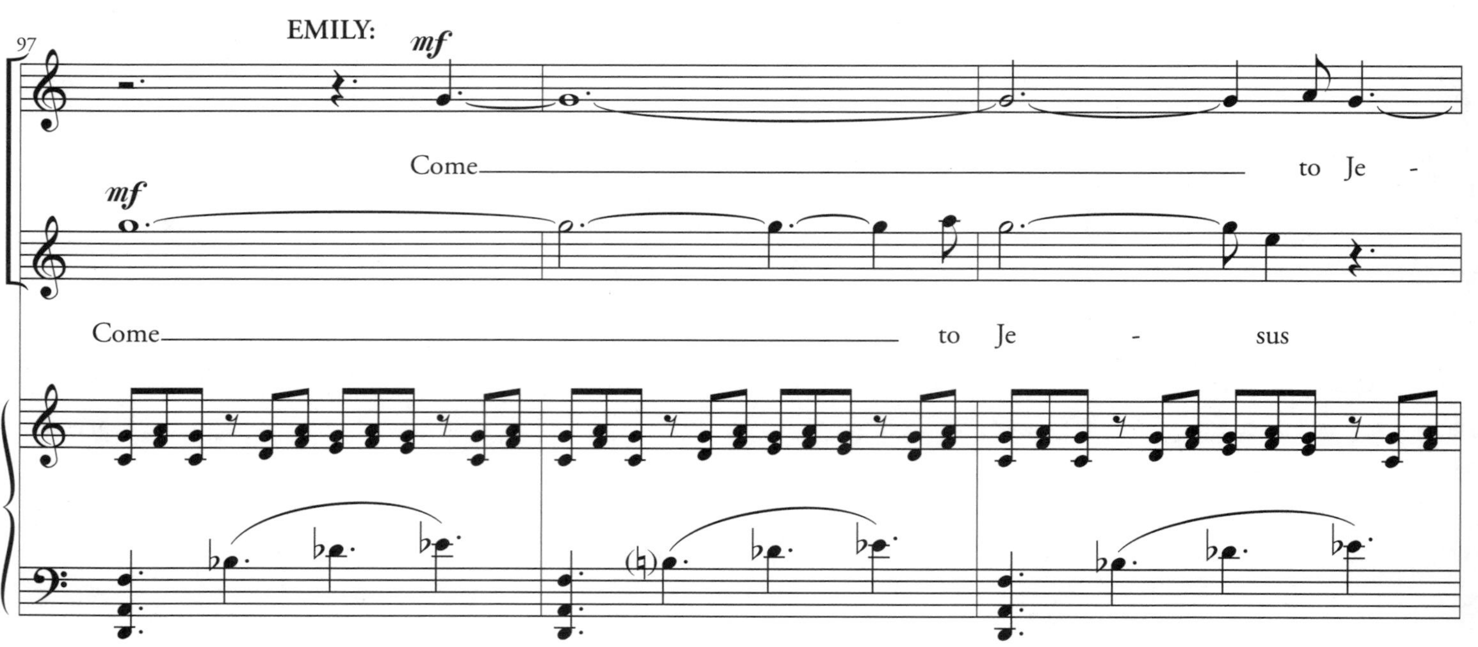
97
EMILY:
mf
Come
to Je -
mf
Come
to Je - sus

100
- sus
Come
Come
to
103
to Je - sus
He will save you
Je - sus
Come to Je -
106
Oh
be - lieve
him
sus just now
Just now come to

109
He is a - ble He'll re - ceive you
Je - sus Come to Je - sus just
112
He will hear you
now He
115
come He'll have mer - cy Come
will hear you

118
He'll for - give you He will cleanse you Come
He will hear you
121
Come to Je - sus just
Come to Je - sus just
f
124
now. Just now come to Je - sus
now. Oh, Oh, be - lieve him He'll re - new you

127
ritard
Come to Je - sus just now
He'll for - give you
ritard
130
He'll for - give you
He'll for - give you
133
Start slower, then accel.
Ah...
Ah...
poco a poco accel.

136
rall.
molto
a tempo
poco a poco dim.
140
Left and right hands rhythmically independent al fine
142

How Can I Lose You?

Music and Lyrics by
Adam Guettel

27
day af - ter day? I look a - round now, you're what I see.
33
Pic - tures of you leav - ing me. No one should al - ways lose.
mf
41
Can't I find some kind of peace? No - bod - y owns the
47
blues, but I have a long term lease. I

53
nev - er know why, I nev - er know when. I'm go - ing a - long, it
59
hap - pens a - gain. I have a blind spot for - ty miles wide.
65
I have a ter - ri - ble weak - ness in - side! That's how I lose you.
71
That's how I lose you.

75
Violin Solo
83
91
I was an - oth - er girl,
joy - ous and hap - py and
mf
97
free.
She was a per - fect pearl,

103
when did she turn in - to me?
107
How can I lose you? You're all that I had. What did I say, now?
113
How was I bad? Who can I turn to? Where will I go?
119
How can I live now, mis - sing you so? How can you leave me? You're

Slower, rubato
all that I know!
Oh!
That's how I lost you!
That's how I al - ways lost you.
That's how I'll al - ways lose you...
In tempo
Violin Solo
Oh.

The Great Highway

Music and Lyrics by
Adam Guettel

Freely

17
p
Ah
Ah
Ah
p
Ah
Ah
p
21
p
Ah
Ah
Ah
Ah
p
Ah
Ah
Ah
Ah
p
Ah
Ah
Ah
Ah
p
Ah
Ah
Ah
Ah
p
Ah
Ah
Ah
Ah
8va

24
f
Ah
Ah
Ah
Ah
Ah
loco
26
p
Oo
Oo
Oo
Oo
Oo
Oo
Oo
Oo
Oo
Oo
p

There's a Land

Music and Lyrics by Adam Guettel
Lyrics adapted from
The Temple Trio, Hymn Edition, 1886

(If segueing from "The Great Highway", omit bars 1-3)

f

mf

WOMAN 1

f

There's a land of pure de - light where Saints im - mor - tal reign.

WOMAN 2

E - ter - nal day ex - cludes the night and pleas - ures ban - ish pain.

WOMEN 1 & 2
There ev - er - last - ing spring a - bides and
nev - er with-'ring flowers. Death like a nar - row sea di - vides this
heav-en - ly land from ours
MAN 3
from ours
ALL
mp
But a

25
lit-tle di-vide
f
ff
28
MAN 1
mf
But a lit-tle di-vide
But a nar-row sea
there
f
mf
sim.
31
is a land
a-wait-ing me
But a blink be-yond
our world-ly
34
care
on joy-ful wing I'll trav-el there

40
ff
land
Oh!
wait - ing me
But a blink be - yond
our world - ly
care
on
land
Oh!
cresc.
ff

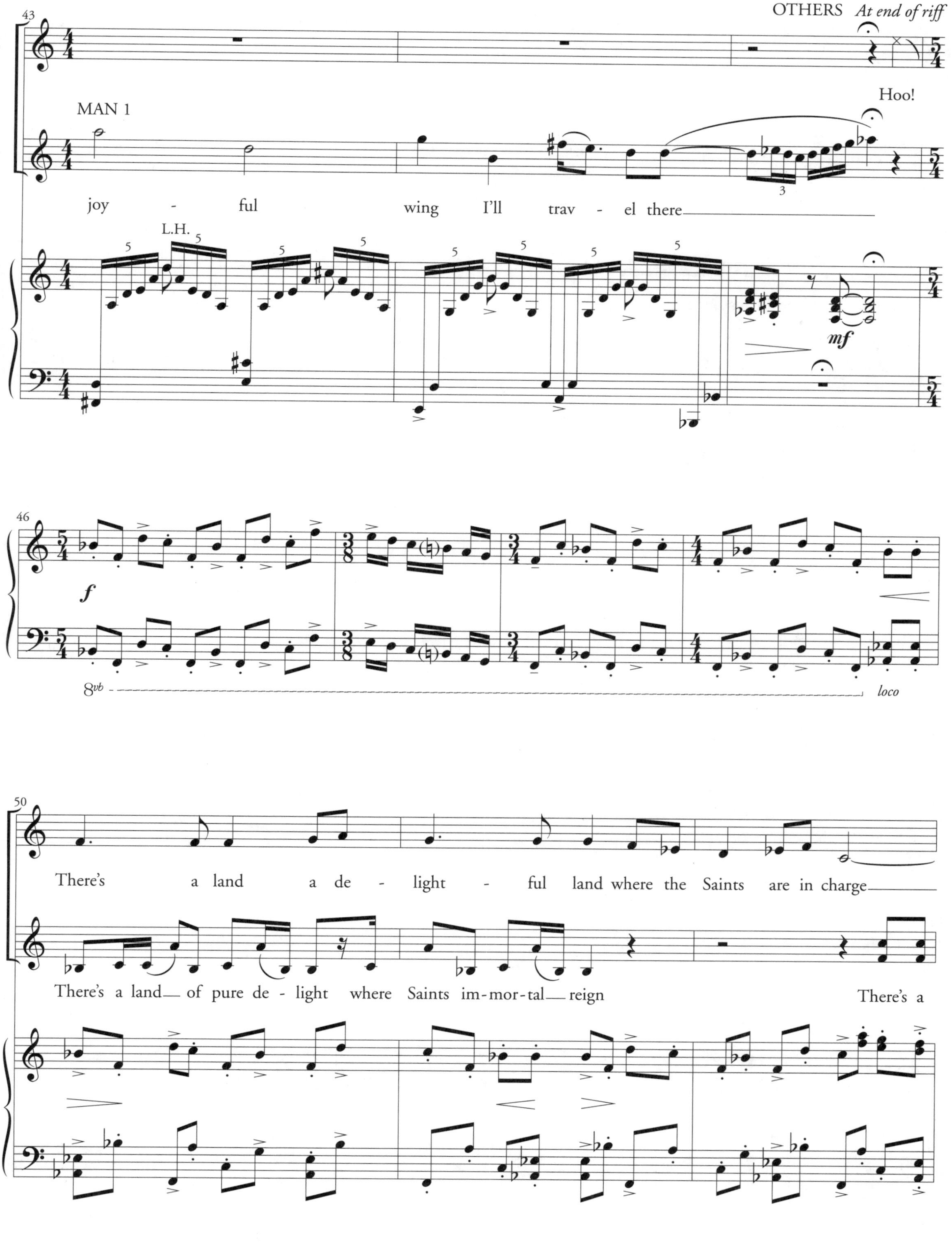

43

OTHERS *At end of riff*

Hoo!

MAN 1

joy - ful wing I'll trav - el there

L.H.

mf

46

f

8vb

loco

53
WOMEN 1 & 3, MAN 1
E - ter - nal day where we laugh and play all the
WOMAN 2, MAN 3
land E - ter - nal day ex-cludes the night and pleas-ures ban-ish pain
MAN 2
Come on, come in it's quite a gar-den.

56
time There ev - er - last - ing spring a - bides and
There's a land There ev - er - last - ing spring a - bides and
I'm tel-ling you it's like a gar - den!

59
(ALL)
nev - er with-'ring flowers
Death like a nar - row sea di - vides this
61
heav - en - ly land from ours
WOMAN 1
from ours
WOMAN 1, MAN 1
64
ff
There's a land
There's a land
Loo loo loo loo loo la
WOMAN 2, MAN 2 (8vb)
Glo - ri - o - so!
Si - a - mo for - tun - a - ti!
WOMAN 3, MAN 3
ff
There's a land
There's a land
There's a
ff

67
li Loo loo la li la li la li loo There's a land
Ness'un per-i - co-lo qui. Mag-ni - fi-ca - tum!
land There's a land There's a land
3
(♮)
70
MAN 1 mf
But a lit-tle di-vide But a nar-row sea there
f
mf
sim.
73
is a land a - wait-ing me But a blink be-yond our world-ly
3

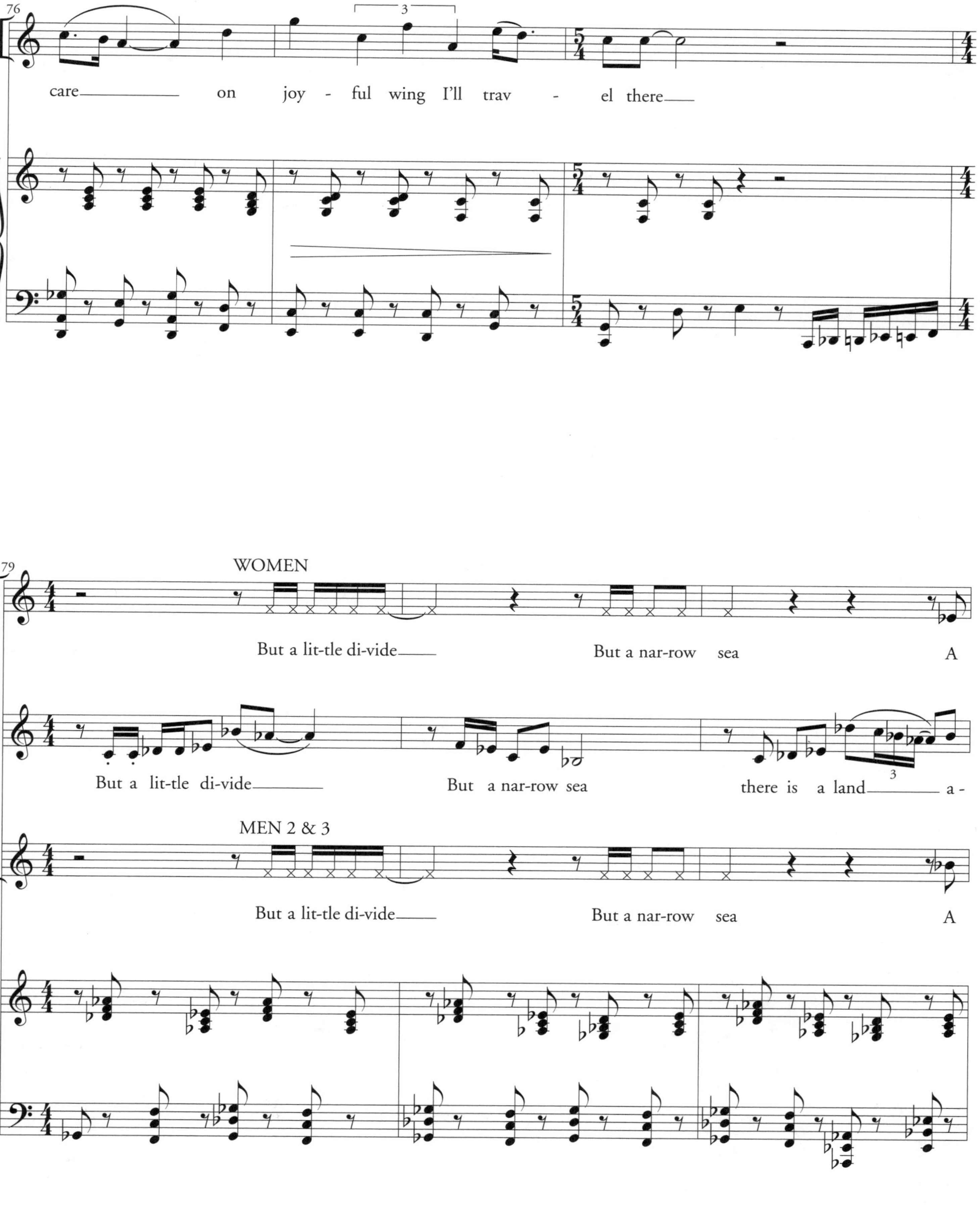

79

WOMEN

But a lit-tle di-vide But a nar-row sea A

But a lit-tle di-vide But a nar-row sea there is a land a-

3

MEN 2 & 3

But a lit-tle di-vide But a nar-row sea A

82

land

Oh!

wait - ing me But a blink be - yond our world - ly care on

land

Oh!

cresc.

ff

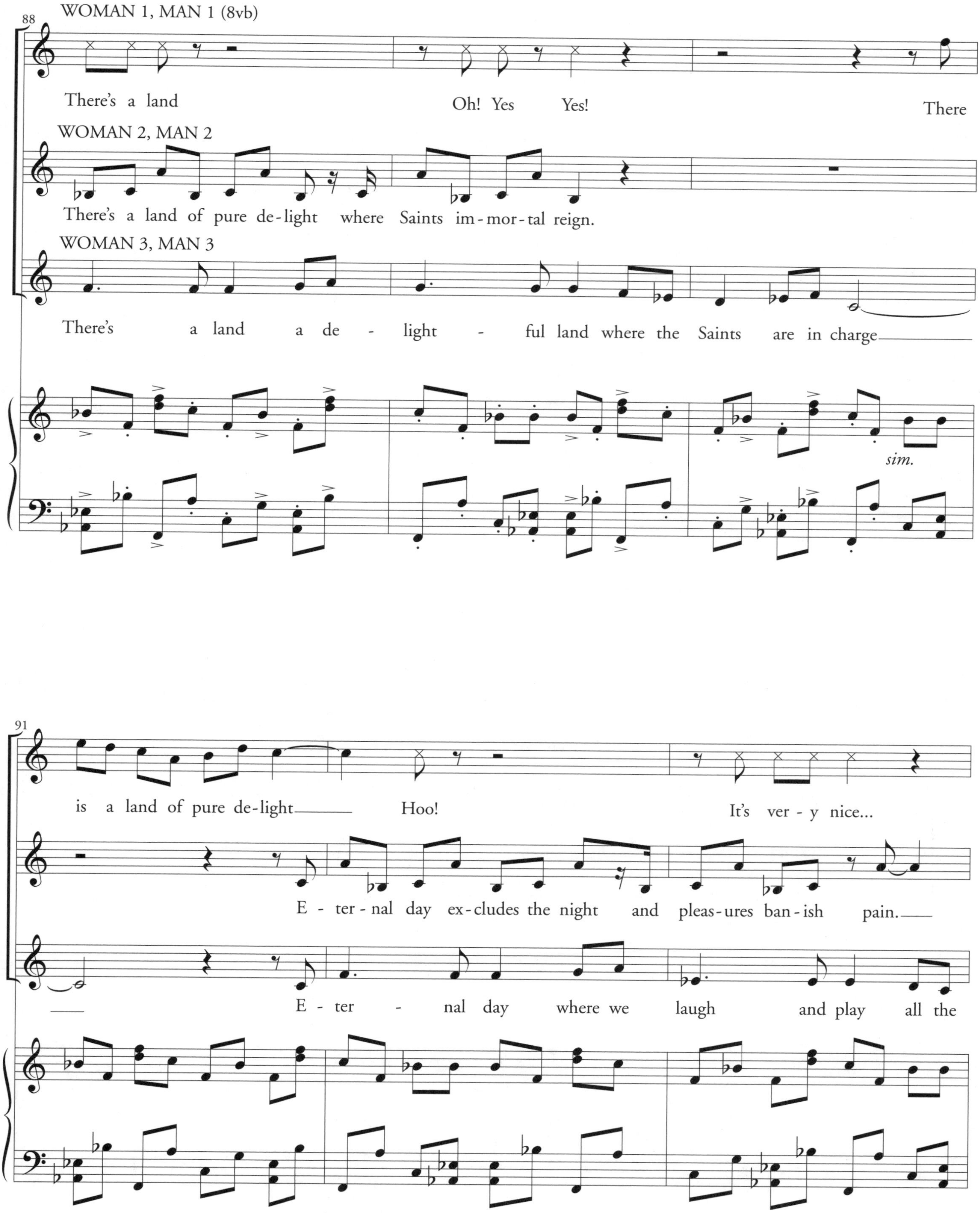

88

WOMAN 1, MAN 1 (8vb)

There's a land Oh! Yes Yes! There

WOMAN 2, MAN 2

There's a land of pure de-light where Saints im-mor-tal reign.

WOMAN 3, MAN 3

There's a land a de - light - ful land where the Saints are in charge

sim.

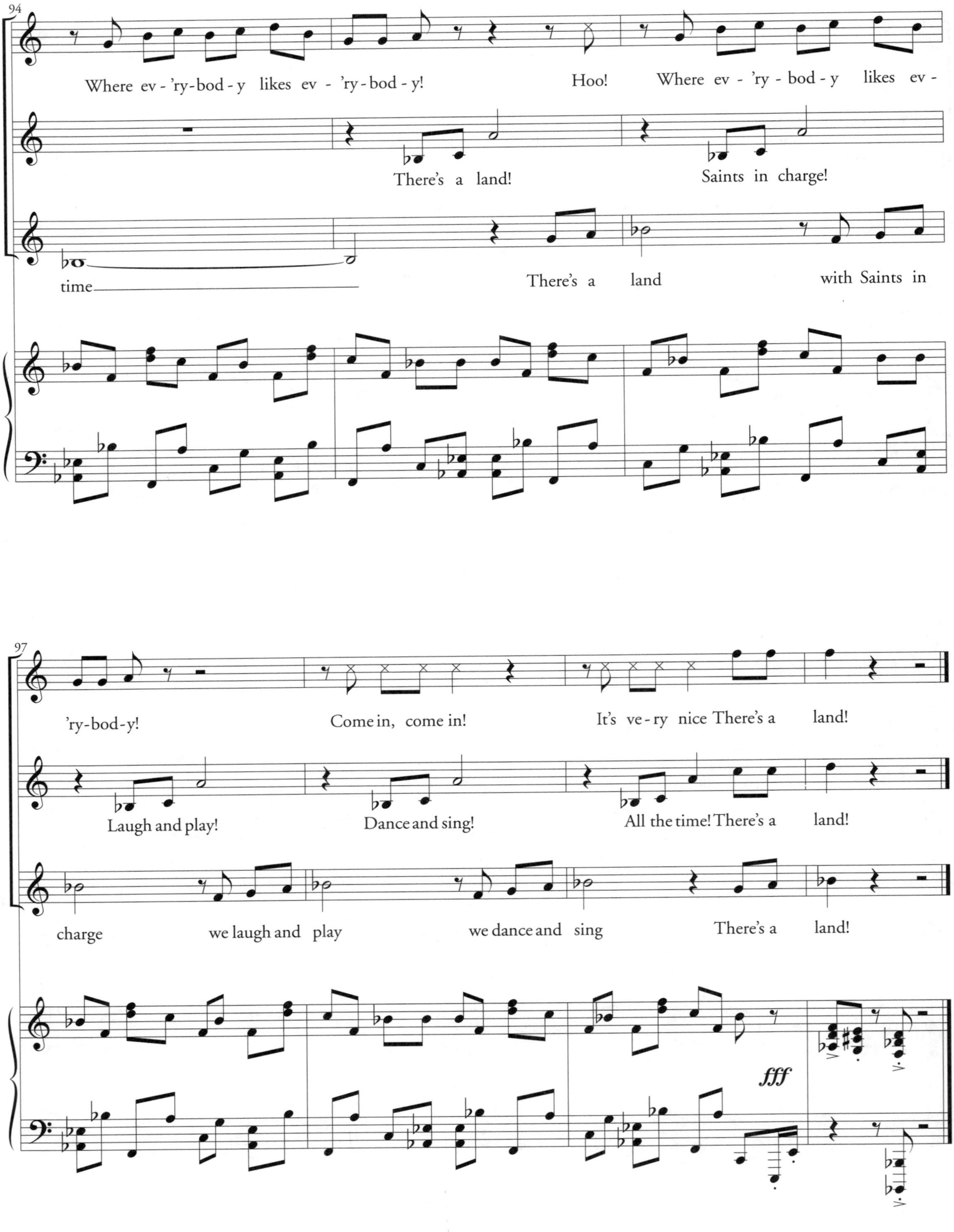

97

'ry-bod-y! Come in, come in! It's ve-ry nice There's a land!

Laugh and play! Dance and sing! All the time! There's a land!

charge we laugh and play we dance and sing There's a land!

fff

There's a Shout

Music and Lyrics by Adam Guettel
Lyrics adapted from
The Temple Trio, Hymn Edition, 1886

26
shout in the land like the shout of old Hal - le-lu-jah praise his name for the
30
crown of his glor - y we now be-hold Praise, oh praise his name
34
Room for the mil - lions There's room for all
38
Hal - le - lu - jah, praise his name

42
Come to the ban - quet
Great and small
Oh praise

46
Oh praise his name
There's a shout in the camp for the
f

51
King of Kings Hal - le - lu - jah praise his name
while we
CHORUS:
Sing Hal - le - lu - jah!

54
drink from the rock of the liv-ing springs Praise, oh praise his name There's a
Shout! Shout it out!
58
shout in the camp while our souls re-peat Hal - le-lu-jah praise his name there is
Sing Hal-le-lu - jah...
62
room for the world at the Sav-ior's feet Praise, praise, praise, praise, praise praise

66
his name
mp
70
74
Room for the mil - lions There's room for all
mp
78
Sing Hal-le-lu - jah, praise his name
Sing!
Praise His name Praise His name now

82
Come to the ban - quet
Great and small
Oh praise
Oo
oo
oo
oo
86
Oh praise
his
name
There's a
Oh, praise
Yes, praise
Praise His name.
There's a
90
shout in the camp for the
King of Kings
Hal - le - lu - jah praise his name
shout!
Hal -
f

93
while we drink from the rock of the liv-ing springs
-le-lu-jah praise His name.
96
Praise, oh praise his name
There's a
Praise Him, Praise Him, Praise Him.
98
shout in the camp while our souls re-peat Hal-

100
- le - lu - jah praise his name
there is
There is
102
room for the world at the Sav - ior's feet
room for the world...
104
Praise, praise, praise, praise, praise, praise!
Praise!
ff

Awaiting You

Music and Lyrics by
Adam Guettel

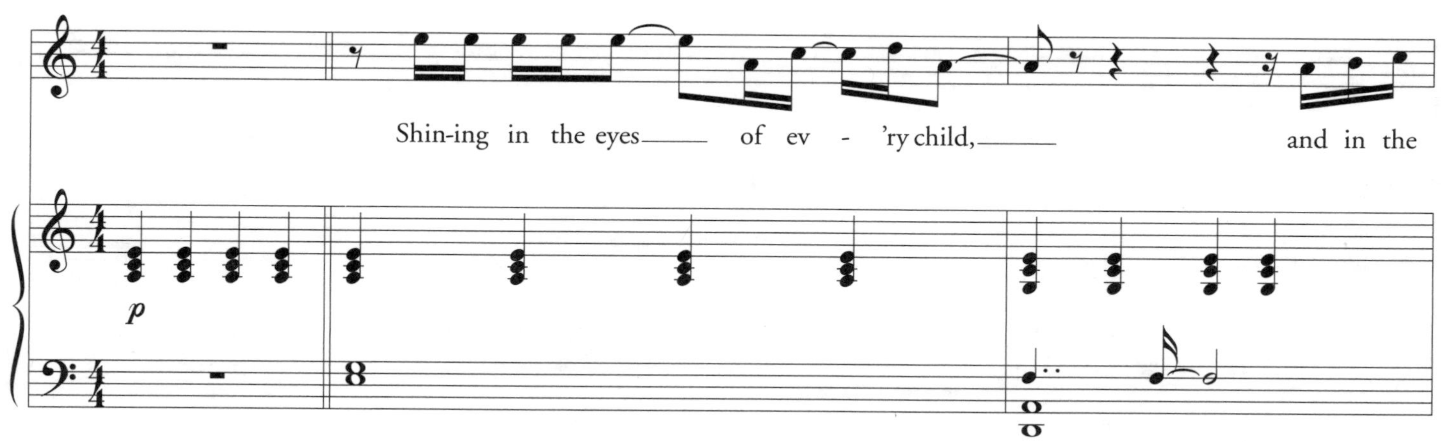

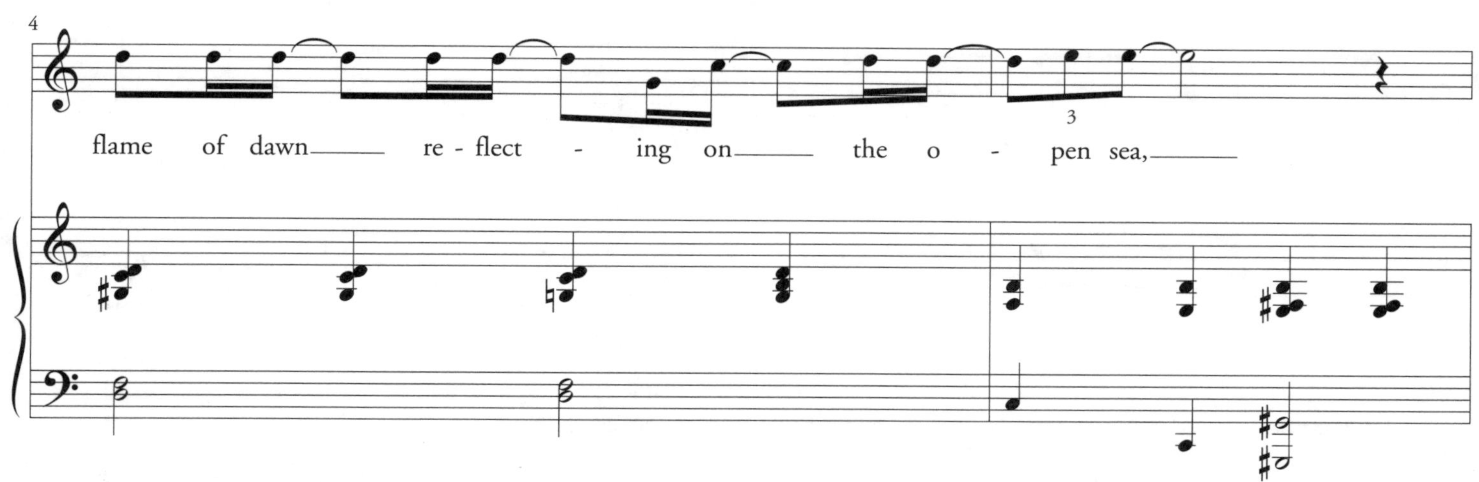

10
But what a-bout the child who can - not breathe?
3
Or the
12
gen - tle sage who won't see the age of thir-ty-two?
3
14
Then what is reign - ing from a - bove?
I am
mf
f
8vb
16
- a - wait - ing, I am a - wait - ing you.
p
mf
p

19
Light it all and burn it to the ground! Go a-head and let your thun-der sound.
f
8vb
21
Let me watch my loves and my teach-ers slow-ly fade a-way.
rit.
colla voce
23
I'll just have to wait an-oth-er day. May-be "In God we trust": just a luck-
p
(8vb)
a tempo
25
-y charm. May-be faith is on-ly hop-ing that we will
8vb

27
rise a-new.
And so I rise and so I stand.
mf
f
(8vb)
29
I am a-wait-ing you.
Oh,
rit.
ff
p
8vb
32
I will still be stand-ing here a-wait-ing you.
a tempo
decresc.
pp
ff
35
Light it all and burn it to the ground!
Go a-head and let your thun-der sound.
ff

37
Let me watch my loves and my teach - ers slow - ly fade a - way.
decresc.
8vb
mf
Vocalise solo
39
I'll just have to wait an - oth - er day.
mf
(8vb)
41
8vb
43
And so I rise, and so I stand.
(8vb)

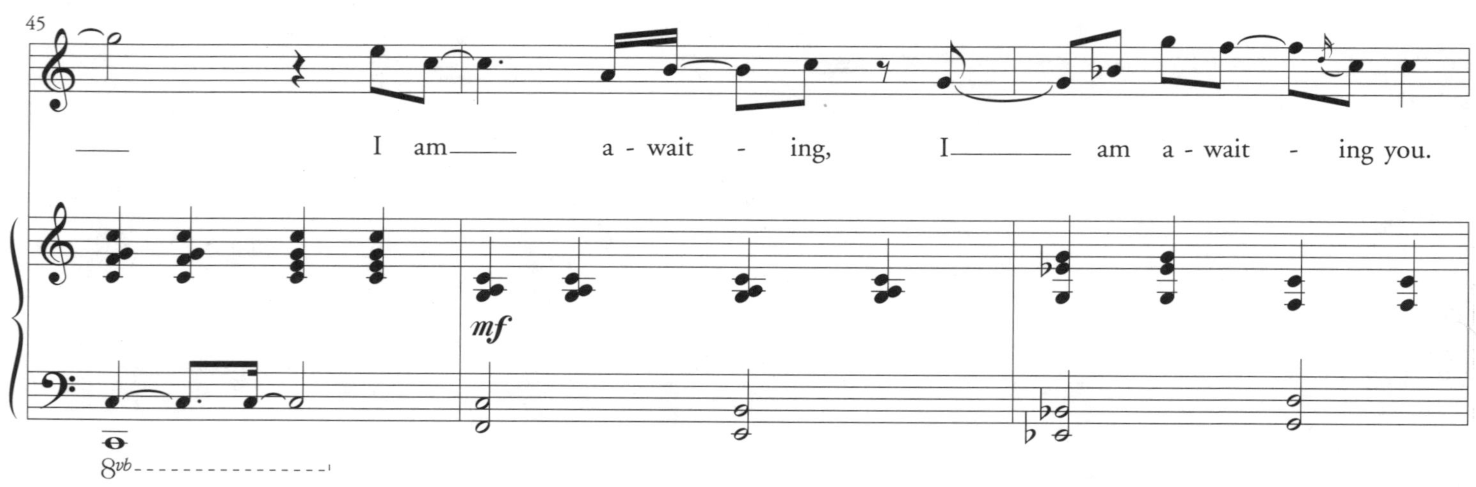
45
I am a - wait - ing, I am a - wait - ing you.
mf
8vb

48
A - wait - ing you. Oh, I will still be stand - ing here a - wait -
rit.
a tempo
8vb
loco

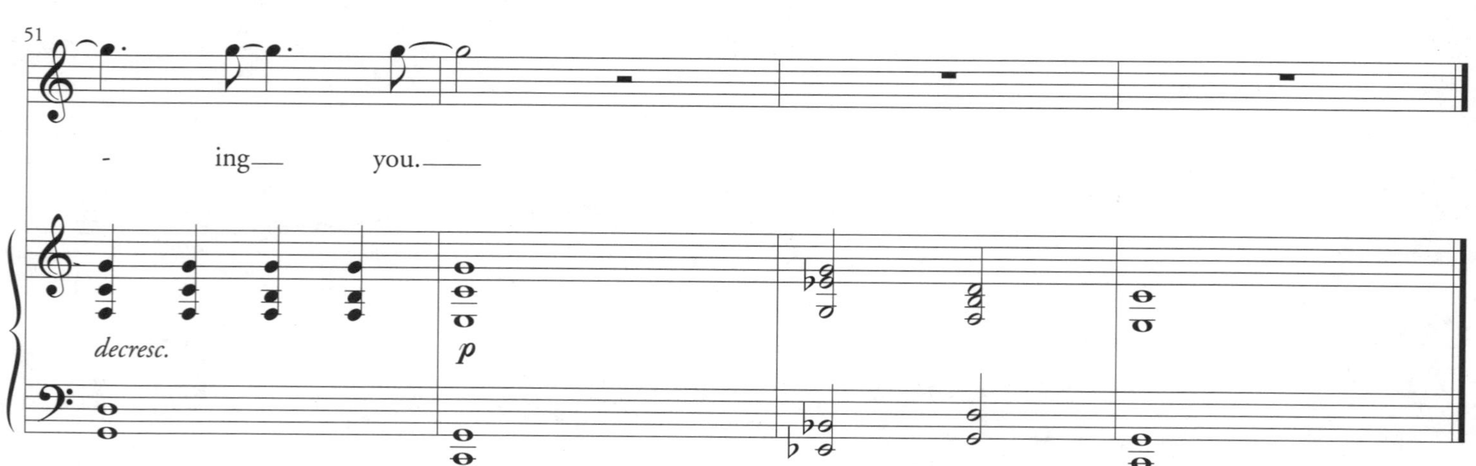
51
- ing you.
decresc.
p